Meditation 101

How Anyone Can Easily Learn to Meditate Even if You Can't Sit Still

Max Fischwell

Liability Disclaimer

By reading this document, you assume all risks associated with using the advice given below, with a full understanding that you, solely, are responsible for anything that may occur as a result of putting this information into action in any way, and regardless of your interpretation of the advice.

You further agree that our company cannot be held responsible in any way for the success or failure of your business as a result of the information presented below. It is your responsibility to conduct your own due diligence regarding the safe and successful operation of your business if you intend to apply any of our information in any way to your business operations.

Terms of Use

You are given a non-transferable, "personal use" license to this product. You cannot distribute it or share it with other individuals.

Also, there are no resale rights or private label rights granted when purchasing this document. In other words, it's for your own personal use only.

Meditation 101

How Anyone Can Easily Learn to Meditate Even if You Can't Sit Still

About the Author

Max Fischwell is about improving his life in various ways, and loves to share what he has accomplished by writing books so that his readers can learn to improve themselves as well.

One of his favorite past-times is to stay fit both mentally as wells as physically. Therefore his favorite endeavers that he has recently embarked upon is practicing yoga and meditation.

Max Fischwell loves Yoga as it can keep you fit physically as well as mentally. However since meditation is an important aspect of yoga, Max Fischwell has taken a profound interest in studying meditation and loves practicing it, as it also has great benefits mentally by itself.

As of right now Max Fischwell is in the process of maintaining his health from cardio and yoga and always looking for other ways he can educate and improve himself on.

Table of Contents

Meditation: What is it and Why Should I Care?

Meditation is the simply the transformation of the mind into a deeper state of self-awareness. Its practices are techniques that encourage the development of concentration, clarity, and calm in seeing the true nature of the world. It involves a quiet and focused state through which an individual becomes peaceful, yet invigorated. There are a number of proven physical, mental, and spiritual benefits that result from engaging in meditation, which will all be explored throughout this book. By engaging in meditation, the individual can cultivate a more positive way of living and form a completely new understanding of their life.

History of Meditation

Although recorded history on meditation is rather scarce, its roots are known to travel back to the ancient world. Over 5000 years ago, meditation evolved into a structured practice in Indian scriptures referred to as tantras. Buddha, one of the major proponents in the history of the practice, first spread his teachings around 500 BC. Meditation spread far and wide across the Asian continent, resulting in separate cultures adopting their own forms. Buddhist and Hindu meditation practices are still the most popular to this day. Thousands of years later, in the mid-20th century, meditation gained popularity in Western society after research found the multitude of benefits associated with the techniques.

Physical Health Benefits

Meditation has been proven through extensive research and studies to significantly lower blood pressure. People who meditate regularly also show boosts in immune system functioning, mostly because the immune system is less likely to become activated during a stressful situation. Meditation is useful if an individual has a chronic medical condition, especially those that are worsened by stress. Some of the health conditions to which meditation has been linked include high blood pressure, cancer, anxiety disorders, chronic pain, high cholesterol, substance abuse, allergies, and heart disease.

Through the many breathing exercises associated with meditation, there is an improved flow of air being pushed into the lungs. This is beneficial for all people, but most especially those who are chronic sufferers of asthma. The deep rest decreases the metabolic rate, lowers the heart rate, and decreases muscle tension.

Therefore, those who have trouble with insomnia are able to fall asleep more easily and sleep soundly without waking up often. This leads to increased levels of energy throughout the day, which will make the individual more alert and ready to take on what life throws their way. Best of all, those who meditate regularly have been found to have a younger biological age than their birthday suggests. Below is a list of some of the most common health benefits you can experience from meditation.

- Decrease in blood pressure
- Better blood flow
- Decrease in heart rate
- A smaller amount of sweat
- Slower breathing rate
- A reduced amount of angst
- Decrease in blood cortisol levels
- Additional feelings of health
- Less stress
- Greater relaxation

Mental Health Benefits

Meditation is often used today as a method for treating psychological disorders such as anxiety, stress, and depression. When practicing meditation, the heart and breathing rate slow down, the blood pressure normalizes, and oxygen is used more efficiently. This causes the adrenal glands to produce less of the hormone cortisol, which reverses the stress response. Not only is meditation linked with a feeling of being less stressed, but stress is literally lowered in the body. The body is able to balance its own neurochemical system to reduce disorder systems. Therefore, meditation causes decreased nervousness, moodiness, tendency to worry, and irritability. There is an excellent reason why meditation has been practiced for literally thousands of years - it helps individuals transform their lives. Most people are aware of the physical benefits of meditation, including reduced high blood pressure, decreased headaches, and improved immune system functioning.

However, many research studies have found tremendous links between meditation and a multitude of mental benefits as well. Practicing meditation helps to lower the breathing rate, find inner peace, and clear errant thoughts from the mind for complete promotion of mental healing. In this section I will go into more detail on some of the many mental health benefits one can achieve from meditation.

Decreases Anxiety and Stress

More and more research evidence is being discovered nearly every year to support the clear association between meditation and decreased levels of both anxiety and stress. For instance, in 2007, a study published in the Proceedings of the National Academy of Sciences journal by University of Oregon researchers found that participating in the body-mind training of meditation actually helps the human body to physiologically lessen the release of cortisol, which is often dubbed the steroid stress hormone. As a result, the study found that college student participants experienced lower levels of stress, anxiety, and even fatigue, compared to those not meditating.

Based on this it should be safe to conclude that meditation can help college students deal better with the challenges presented by college such as handling the pressure from mid-term and final exams or having to write a major report. Obviously when able to handle the stress associated with college students can focus better and ultimately get better grades as a result. Also in the year of 2008, the Journal of American College Health published a study with similar results that demonstrated how meditation has the power to reduce stress, as well as enhance forgiveness.

Recently, researchers from the Wake Forest Baptist Medical Center published an even more detailed study in the Social Cognitive and Affective Neuroscience journal. The study involved 15 participants who reported normal stress levels without a history of anxiety disorders or participating in meditation. To begin with, the participants received brain scans to track their normal brain activity and anxiety levels. After training the participants in just four 20-minute meditation classes, the researchers followed up with another brain scan. The study found that meditation was found to impact the ventromedial prefrontal cortex of the brain, which is the part of the brain that is responsible for controlling worries. Therefore, participant anxiety levels were lowered by up to 39 percent after learning meditation practices.

In March of 2013, the journal of Health Psychology published more supporting evidence for a distinct relationship between mindfulness and stress. Conducted by postdoctoral researchers at the

University of California, the study followed 57 participants who spent three months at a Shamatha meditation retreat. At the start of the study, all participants had their levels of cortisol measured through a saliva test and individually self-rated their mindfulness levels on a designated scale. Not only did the researchers discover much higher ratings for mindfulness at the end of the retreat, but test results also demonstrated dramatic decreases in the level of cortisol.

While it is beneficial for all individuals to decrease their levels of anxiety, it is even more crucial for those who are battling Post-Traumatic Stress Disorder (PTSD). Whether the disorder is the result of war, abuse, or other forms of violence, the journal Depression and Anxiety has proven that meditation could be the answer. In the study, PTSD patients from a VA outpatient clinic underwent eight-weeks of cognitive therapy treatment that was based on meditation. After the end of the program, the researchers from the University of Michigan found that 73 percent of veterans who were involved in the meditation therapy had improvements in stress and anxiety symptoms of the disorder, compared to only 33 percent in standard treatment.

Relieves Depression

Depression is a severe mental illness that nearly 19 million American adults are living with on a daily basis. Although there are anti-depressant medications and therapy techniques that have proven effective, research findings indicate that meditation may be just as beneficial for relieving the crippling symptoms of depression. Not to mention of that fact that you don't have to worry about side effects one may experience when taking medications. The American College of Rheumatology published a study in 2007 that found mindfulness meditation to be successful at alleviating the depressive symptoms of women suffering from fibromyalgia. During the eight-week study, the 91 female participants were led by a licensed clinical psychologist through meditation training. In the end, symptoms of depression improved significantly for all patients over the three assessments versus the participants in the control group.

Research by the University of Exeter and the Mindfulness in Schools Project (MiSP) also has provided evidence that meditation is not only beneficial for adults but for kids as well. In the study, the researchers taught 256 students between the ages of 12 and 16 mindfulness meditation techniques throughout nine different lessons. Even for the most cynical of adolescent age groups, the results found that children and teenagers who are taught meditation are less likely to develop depressive or mood disorder symptoms. After a three-month follow up interview, around 80 percent of the participants reported still using the meditation techniques and seeing boosts in their academic performance.

Improves Focus and Concentration

For those that are having a hard time staying focused in their lives, research studies demonstrate that meditation may help. In the 2010 study published in the Psychological Science journal, thirteen researchers at the University of California Davis sought to find solid evidence of increased concentration among individuals who meditated. During a three-month meditation retreat, the researchers chose 60 meditation enthusiasts to participate in concentration tests at the beginning, halfway through, and at the end. Compared to the wait-list control group, the active meditators were more focused and more accurate when completing the concentration tests.

Although most people cannot afford to spend the time or money to attend a retreat and meditate for six hours daily, it is important to note that the same increased focus benefits were found in shorter studies too. For instance, the researchers at the University of North

Carolina Charlotte found in past research that college students were able to improve concentration within just four days.

After participants underwent four days of meditation training for only 20 minutes each day, they showed significant improvement in concentration and associated critical cognitive skills to boost their cognition. Throughout the intense battery of behavioral tests examining their mood, visual attention, vigilance, memory, and focus, students who received meditation training achieved statistically significant higher scores. Therefore not only does meditation help college students with dealing with stress from college but also at the same times helps them to focus and concentrate on their studies as well. No wonder why these students are able to perform better.

Increases Happiness and Self-Confidence

As part of human nature, it is normal for people to become subjective when examining themselves and their personalities. However, one of the best ways to take off the rose-colored glasses is through mindfulness meditation. In a study published by the journal Perspectives on Psychological Science, researchers discovered that meditation practices help individuals to become more aware of their inner being without the negative bias emotions. Participants reported higher levels of emotional stability, more self-awareness, less anxiety, and increased levels of positive emotions related to their self-confidence.

In another study by the Laboratory for Affective Neuroscience at the University of Wisconsin, researchers studied the brain imaging scans of monks who regularly practice meditation. The surprising results discovered that the brain circuitry for long-term meditators is different than those who do not meditate. Normally, when individuals are upset or sad, the amygdale and the right prefrontal cortex of the brain become active on brain scans. On the other hand, the left prefrontal cortex becomes increasingly active when people are in a positive, happy mood. Interestingly enough, the meditating monks exhibited especially high activity in the left prefrontal cortex, thus showing evidence that meditation can increase happiness.

Elderly adults are among the highest at risk for suffering extreme loneliness and unhappiness, which can lead to heart risks and at times premature death. In the Brain, Behavior, & Immunity journal, a July 2012 study shed some light on the latest tool to help the elderly fight against loneliness – meditation. For the research, 40 participants between 55 and 85 years old underwent eight weeks of mindfulness meditation at home for a half hour daily. After the program was completed, the results showed significant decreases in loneliness, as well as reduced inflammation that could lead to heart or brain diseases.

In addition to the main benefits mentioned in this article, meditation has been scientifically linked to increased intelligence, stronger decision making skills, higher memory functioning, and even slow aging. In fact, a study by the International Journal of Neuroscience discovered that people who have meditated for five or more years are 12 years younger than their chronological age!

Many individuals who engage in meditation are trying to break an unhealthy habit, such as drinking or smoking. These practices can help people accomplish this through detaching the emotion from the action. Meditation improves the communication that people have with themselves, which gives them added control over what they think and do. Increased understanding of the thought processes in the mind will help remedy and even prevent mental health concerns.

Those that meditate are more likely to report feelings of vitality, rejuvenation, emotional control, and self-esteem. Increased amounts of confidence and emotional well-being will go on to further improve the individual's relationships with other people and him/herself. Meditation has also been linked to increased creativity, intelligence, concentration, and moral reasoning because it allows a deeper state of mindfulness. Overall, research has proven that meditation can have significant improvements on various areas of mental health for an enduring, more positive life.

Spiritual Benefits

Meditation brings individuals closer to the heart of God. Not necessarily trying to get religious, but there is no doubt that those who believe in some Supreme Being or who practice religion can get more in touch with their religious side through meditation. Through the process of emptying and silencing the mind, people are able to experience a deeper communion where they can discover power beyond this world. The peace of mind leads to a heightened awareness of the inner self. The ability to look within, beyond the mind, body, and personality lets the person become transcended.

Here the individual is able to find one's true being and form a deep bond with the Supreme Being. People who meditate often report feeling the presence of God within them, while their feet are still planted on the Earth. However, even if you don't believe in God meditation will still help you spiritually. You would simply just simply replace God with the Universe. In fact some look as meditation as becoming one with the Universe. Therefore meditation is a process of self-realization and allows for a spiritual reawakening no matter who you are or what you believe.

In today's world, it is easy to get too caught up in the stresses of daily life. Therefore, you should take time out of your busy schedule to get away and have some alone time. Putting your mind at peace for just 20 short minutes a day will cause noticeable changes in your behavior, health, attitude, and thinking patterns. Many problems will just disappear, while others will become easier to cope with.

However, you don't necessarily need to even start out with 20 minutes. Even if you can only do 5 minutes a day starting out you will still eventually start to notice some positive changes within you. Start out with whatever you are comfortable with, and you can build upon that as time goes on. The last thing you want to do is make meditation so daunting that you find it a chore to do. Meditation should not be a chore. In fact it should be the opposite. It should be an escape from the daily mundane chores and duties that consume most of your life.

Meditating should be something that you look forward to everyday. You may not feel this way at first but that's okay. That's actually what this book is intended for. To help you overcome the most common obstacles people have with meditation and to make it enjoyable as possible. That is why you may want to just start out with only a few minutes a day. This way it may not seem so daunting at first.

However, as time goes on, you should start to notice it getting easier and easier and will have no trouble with increasing your time to 10, 15 or even 20 minutes at a time. In fact there has been many times where I would plan on only meditating for may be 10 minutes and I would get so lost in my deep and peaceful state of mind that 20 minutes would end up passing without me realizing it. Therefore if you are limited on time, it may not be a bad idea to have a timer set for whatever time you plan on spending on meditating.

By the end of this book, hopefully you will be convinced that meditating is not only very beneficial, but also a very enjoyable process as well. And no doubt once you try it a few times and notice how calm and peaceful you feel right afterwards it certainly will be. So, find a quiet place, relax your body, silence your mind, and let the healing power of meditation overtake your body.

So How Should I Start Out if I Never Meditated Before?

Meditation is a method of exercising the psyche, comparable to the way that fitness is a method to exercising the body. Also just like regular exercise, numerous meditation methods are present.

In Buddhist tradition, the word "meditation" is comparable to our word, "sports." It represents a grouping of actions, not just a specific detail. Diverse meditative exercises have need of dissimilar intellectual abilities, much like diverse sports have need of distinctive bodily abilities.

It is very trying for a beginner to be seated for hours with a clear head. Most of the time, the simplest approach to commence meditating is by concentrating on your inhalation.

This meditation exercise is an excellent introduction

to meditation techniques.

1. Sit or lie restfully.

2. Close your eyes.

3. Make no attempt to influence the inhalation; just respire innately.

4. Direct your concentration on the inhalation and on how the figure moves with every breath. Observe the movement of your form as you respire. Witness your upper body, rib cage, and abdomen. Again, make no attempt to manage your inhalation and exhalation; merely direct your concentration. If your psyche meanders, merely return your attention back to your inhalation. Keep up this meditation ritual for 2-3 minutes to start off and then attempt to meditate for lengthier amounts of time.

A slightly more advanced meditation practice has to do with fixating on a lone entity. This may possibly consist of observing the inhalation, reciting a solitary word or intonation, gazing at a candle's flickering light, listening to a monotonous gong, or totaling beads on a rosary.

Isochronic Tones

In view of the fact that concentrating the psyche is taxing, a novice may well meditate for merely a small number of minutes and subsequently work on developing into meditating for lengthier periods. However you may just find it too difficult to sit still and get in the right frame of mind to meditate properly and staying focused. One method to assist you in focusing is by using isochronic tones. These tones are an extremely helpful audio-based way of motivating the mind. This technique is a sample of a multifaceted neurological procedure identified as brainwave entertainment.

This allows the assistance of auditory or optical incentives to influence the mind and assist individuals with an assortment of complications. At its plainest stage, an isochronic tone is simply a sound that is being turned on and off quickly. They produce piercing, idiosyncratic beats of reverberation.

When using isochronic tones to help you meditate, you merely transfer your cognizance on the selected entity of concentration every single time you become aware of your thoughts going off on a tangent. As an alternative to following chance ideas, you just let them go. In the course of this method, your adeptness to focus develops.

Mindfulness Meditation

A method that inspires the individual to adhere to drifting observations as they flow through the psyche is mindfulness meditation. The objective is not to become drawn in to the reflections or to form an opinion about them, but merely to be mindful of every single intellectual communication as it takes place. During the course of mindfulness meditation, you will be able to grasp in what way your opinions and emotional states tend to progress in specific collections. As time passes, you can become more conscious of the social propensity to hurriedly consider encounters as "upright" or "corrupt."

Mindfulness meditation is great for beginners for a couple different reasons. Number one it is accepting your thoughts and your environment as the way it is. You don't get frustrated with it but rather accept it as it is. What you will find by doing this is that it will become easier to let your thoughts or sounds around you go and to focus back on whatever you were focusing on such as your breathing.

Another very common challenge many beginners experience when meditating is clearing one's mind. When a beginner tries to meditate they usually will find that their thoughts will become louder and more intense then when they started. Of course this just leads to frustration and when one becomes frustrated with their thoughts, they essentially become more obsessed with them which of course causes them to be even more profound. Needless to say this can really discourage beginners from continuing with meditation.

However with mindfulness meditation you are simply welcoming your thoughts and become more receptive of them. This doesn't mean that you engage with them, but rather you just simply label it as a thought. By labeling the thought and becoming more accepting of the thought occurring you can then simply tell yourself that you can always come back to your thought at a later time if you desire. By becoming less stressed out over thoughts flowing within you, you will find it easier to simply let them go and tune back in to your breathing. This is why this is a great meditative techniques for beginners. I will touch more upon mindfulness meditation later on in this book.

How Long Should I Meditate?

Finding time to meditate with your busy schedule

You understand that your life would improve greatly with daily meditation practice, but you find it difficult to plan it around your busy schedule. Luckily, you don't have to let a busy life keep you from benefiting from meditation. By consistently practicing meditation for even two minutes a day, you will be able to reap the rewards of meditation.

The benefits of daily meditation

By meditating daily, you will see immense benefits in all areas of your life. You will find yourself staying calmer while under pressure in business and relationships. You will be able to analyze the problems in your life without succumbing to anxiety, and you will be able to finally take the path to success. With meditation, you will no longer be held back by your weaknesses; instead, you will be able to overcome them with a clear mind. In order to achieve this calmness and ability to control stress, you need to meditate daily.

Finding time to meditate with a busy schedule

If you have a busy schedule, then you can still find the time to meditate daily for tremendous results. While the optimal time for meditation is 15 minutes, even just two minutes a day will help you to overcome stress. Meditating for any amount of time, whether it's for two minutes or an hour, is beneficial as long as you stick to your new routine. Make sure to keep to your new meditation schedule in order to reap the benefits. If you only meditate once a week, then you cannot expect to reap the various benefits one experiences from meditation.

Quality over quantity

It is important that you take your meditation routine seriously in order to see results. If you only have five minutes to practice, then use those minutes to the fullest in order to advance in your practices. You will be surprised at your progression if you consistently meditate for a few weeks. If you stick to your routine, then you will find yourself calmer and more focused throughout the day.

How to meditate anywhere

While meditating in your own home may be the best option, you can always find a way to get your meditation practice in during a busy day. Take a moment to meditate in the office, or meditate for a moment on your lunch break in order to stay consistent. You can even try meditating while on the bus or train. While being on the bus may not seem ideal for meditation, you will eventually find yourself tuning out the noise around you.

If you have a really busy hectic schedule, you may have to get a little more creative at times. For example maybe on your way home from work you are usually stuck in a traffic jam due to rush hour. If you know that you are going to be stalled for at least a good few minutes then why not practice meditating right then. This would be a good opportunity to practice mindful meditation.

I will go further into that in a later section. Just using this time to focus on your breathing however, will certainly help. You may want to turn your music down, or even play some isochronic tunes if you have them available. Just make sure you keep your eyes open so you can see if traffic starts moving. The last thing you want is to be broken out of your peaceful state of mind by a loud horn honking at you.

Finding the best time to meditate

If you can fit it into your schedule, then try meditating in the morning to start your day on the best foot. You will be able to start the day off with a calm demeanor and a clear head, and you can then meditate again during lunch in order to prolong the benefits. However, this may not be possible due to your busy schedule. Make sure not to stress about waking up earlier to meditate, because reducing stress is one of the main goals of meditation.

While the morning is ideal, it is more important to find a consistent time in your day's schedule. Perhaps you may want to set your alarm clock for five minutes earlier so you can try meditating. The five minutes difference will not have much of any impact on your sleep, but can make a noticeable difference in how you feel when you're ready to start you day. Not to mention you are also more likely to be more energized as well. Or maybe you can try to meditate right before you go to bed. It really doesn't matter when just as long as that you do.

Even by simply finding just a few minutes once or twice a day for meditation, you will still notice positive results. Just find a way to make it ideal for your schedule. By following these tips, you will be able to meditate with any schedule. Make sure to stay consistent with your practice in order to make it worthwhile. Once you are able to manage this, you will find yourself more calm and leading a more productive life due to your meditating practices.

How Should I Sit?

Many of you when starting may wonder if you need to sit a certain way in order to meditate properly. You may want to know about the different positions and which position is best for you. Well I am going to make this as simple as possible. It doesn't matter what position you sit in!

This may seem like an unconventional thing to say, but it really is true. The only thing that really matters is that you are comfortable and preferably you are sitting up with a straight spine. That's really it. But the most important thing is that you are comfortable. So if sitting up straight and erect becomes uncomfortable than go ahead and slouch a little if you have to.

Remember that the main objective when you meditate is to stay focused. It's hard to stay focused when you are uncomfortable or even in pain from trying some of the sitting techniques, such as the full lotus position with both feet on top of your thighs. If you are flexible and like the challenge then go for it, but for most people it just isn't realistic. Remember; meditation is not supposed to be painful, but pleasurable, so if you're sitting position is causing you pain or discomfort than I can tell you that you are simply doing it wrong.

For added comfort you may want to look into purchasing a meditation cushion. I won't go into detail on the different types but some of the most common are the zafu, rectangular cushion and crescent cushion. If you want to find more about these you can just google them online to see which one you may like. Otherwise a pillow will also suffice for most individuals. It's actually what I use and I find it to work great.

Of course as you get a little more advanced you may want to challenge yourself a bit and try some of the more advanced positions or you just may want a few ideas on different sitting positions to try out. Whether this describes you or you are just curious, I went ahead and included some photos of the different common meditation positions with a brief explanation.

Burmese

This position is very ideal for beginners. Unless you are extremely flexible you may find a lot of the other positions very difficult making this option very attractive for most. All it is, is just sitting cross legged with your feet underneath each thigh. Then you just want to sit with your back straight. The hands on your knees are optional though common is not necessary. That's pretty much it with this one.

Seiza

Out of all the positions this is probably one the easiest to implement. The Seiza position was adopted by the Japanese around the 18th century as a customary way to sit in their culture. However, around the 20th centry this practice became much less common, is still pretty popular in many Japanese martial arts, such as Aikido and Kendo, to this day

It is just simply sitting straight up on your knees with your buttocks resting on your heels. The top of your feet then should be resting the floor and your angles slightly pointing outwards. This position is ideal for those who may be very inflexible to the point that the Burmese position may still be a little challenging for them. The only problem with this position is that your knees may get sore after a short while, so instead of doing this one on a hard wood floor like above I would highly recommend a cushion or pillow.

Lotus (Ouch!)

For those of you with crazy flexibility and want to challenge yourself, then you may find the Lotus position appealing. This position is very common in the Buddhist tradition of meditation. The position gets its name from resembling a lotus, a common flower in many parts of Asia.

You may wonder why anyone would want to try this position. Well I can tell you that most people should not, however if you are extremely flexible and able to do it, it is supposed to help with proper breathing. It also helps with stability and also by applying pressure to the lower spinal area may induce relaxation. Also some believe that a lot of the blood flow to the legs is redirected to your abdomen which can help with digestion.

For those that want to try this out I would highly recommend using a zafu cushion, or a least a padded mat as balance and comfort are very important. First, place one foot upon the opposite thigh, with your sole faing as upwards as possible. You want your foot as close to your abdomen as possible. Then simply place your other foot on its opposite thigh so that you are sitting symmetrically. You want to have both knees touching the ground if possible. Your spinal column should now support your torso with minimal muscle involvement. You torso should also be directly above your hips.

If you are able to successfully pull this off than simply congratulate yourself. You are more flexible than probably over 90% of the people in the world. At least in the U.S for sure. Please remember that if you are experiencing pain than you should probably not pursue this. As mentioned earlier pain can distract you from focus and in extreme cases may even cause injury. As stated for most of us this position is simply out of question. However there is a slightly easier version of this that you can try called the half-lotus which I will be showing next, but even this position is not easy.

Half-Lotus

The half-lotus position is simply a modified version of the lotus position. Instead of having both feet on your thigh, you would simply place one foot upon your thigh and the other one underneath. If you can't quite get your foot right on top of your thigh that is okay. As you can see in the picture above as long as it is slightly upon it then you are doing it well. Just try and make sure the sole of your foot is facing upward. With this position instead of sitting symmetrically you would be sitting asymmetrically.

This position is a little bit easier than the regular lotus position, but still not easy for most to pull off. But for those of you who are getting better and more flexible this could be something to work up to. Of course remember to stop if you are experience any pain or discomfort.

These are the most common meditative positions. As mentioned earlier though; you don't have to do any of these if you don't want. Essentially whatever makes you the most comfortable is what you should do. Maybe you want to sit on a chair. I would suggest to try some of the above positions are try and experiment different ways that you can think of on your own. Whatever you can find that makes you the most comfortable with preferably an erect spine than that is really the one you should use.

Mantras:

What Are They and Do I Need to Use Them?

Mantras are medicine for the soul. They are simple chants, phrases, and prayers that are specifically designed to create vibrations that facilitate spiritual growth, healing, and creativity. While mantras are not necessary to meditate it may be a good idea to consider incorporating them into your meditative practices for a couple of reasons. One is that they help your mind stay focused and helps prevents your mind from wondering. Also they can help you obtain a deeper meditative state of mind as well.

The word "mantra" comes from two Sanskrit words; "manas," which means mind, and "trai," which means to "free from." Therefore, mantras are literally tools to

56

free from the mind. For those that are new to meditation, or those that are experts at transformativesilence, mantras can deepen the meditative experience by providing a subtle focus that frees the mind from distractions. The following will explore how to use them, some sample mantras, and how they can end up changing your life.

How Mantras Work

Sanskrit is considered by many linguists to be the ideal language, because correct pronunciation leads to unique vibrations unlike any other. Practitioners of mediation use this vibration in order to connect with the Universe and place into motion whatever is being manifested through the mantra chosen. During a meditative experience, the individual chooses a word or series of words that they will repeat as a mantra. Usually, the person will select a mantra that speaks to them spiritually and elicits a powerful response within them. By repeating the mantra over and over, it is becoming affirmed within the inner soul. The meaning seeps under the surface towards the subconscious.

The meaning flows into the seven chakras of the body, which are the energy processing centers located along the spine and top of the head. Each chakra responds to a specific vibration and the mantras are tools to create a vibrational accord with every center. Imagine a chakra as being an instrument and the mantra a tuning fork. By striking the tuning fork, the instrument comes into resonance with it. This clears out all negative energies that do not share the same vibrational meaning. Thus, the mantra frees the body of negativity and bad habits, and replaces them with more positive ones.

Examples of Mantras

One of the most well-known and universal meditative mantras is OM, the mantra of acceptance and acquiesce. This simple syllable vibrates at 432 Hertz, which is the natural pitch of the Universe. The sound causes energy to gather and flow up the spine; therefore, making it an excellent mantra to prepare the energy for later movement in the meditative experience. OM helps individuals to accept their higher self and let the energy flow through without any hindrances. Increasing or decreasing the frequency of the sound can create changes that will coincide with the Universe and keep still the thoughts of the mind.

Another powerful mantra is Om Namah Shivaya. This phrase translates to "I honor the divinity within myself." If you are familiar with the book Eat Pray Love by Elizabeth Gilbert, you have heard of this mantra, which her Guru gifted her with. She affectionately refers to it as the "Amazing Grace of Sanskrit." And, the energy in this mantra is truly amazing for building self-confidence. The mantra helps to remind the individual that they are made up of divine energy; therefore, they must treat themselves accordingly.

Om Gum Ganapatayei Namah is a popular mantra within Hindu teachings. Ganesh is the god of wisdom and success, who destroys all obstacles. The mantra is to be said as a prayer to the god for blessings and protection. It is the most powerful for individuals who are going through a tough challenge in their lives and need some guidance.

How Mantras Transform

Spending a few hours chanting mantras can have a remarkable effect. The vibrations of the mantras allow stimulation of the chakras, which enables a more relaxed state of consciousness in the mind. The mind will become freer, calmer, and more easily void of distractions. Mantras work in a way that leaves the body elevated into a spiritually altered state of being. They are powerful tools for healing, as they energize the life inside of the individual. Many healers use these mantra techniques for healing diseases or health conditions, which demonstrates the great power source here.

Choose the mantras that you intuitively connect with and feel you need to embrace within your meditative experience. All of them may not be necessary, because you may be very healthy in some respects and not in others. Pick mantras that resonate with your individual spiritual needs and begin incorporating it into your meditation. Within some time, you will feel the power of the healing energies run through your body and change your life for the better.

What if I Can't Sit Still?

If you are like I was when I first starting out in meditation, one of your main concerns may be that you absolutely cannot stand the idea of having to sit still for even a few minutes. If you have ADHD or find yourself to be really restless for whatever reason, you just may find the concept of meditation to be a somewhat daunting task. Fortunately, however meditation doesn't necessarily have to be just sitting still with your eyes closed for 15 minutes. Believe it or not you can actually meditate while you are walking which may be ideal for those of us who sometimes struggle to sit still at times.

Walking meditation is often as profound as meditation while sitting, plus it has the advantage of combining the meditative experience with physical activity. In fact, it is much easier to become aware of and pay attention to the body when it is in motion, rather than sedentary, which makes it easier to implement when you are a beginner. It lets you become more present in the body and in the moment. The simple movement of alternating steps from the left to the right foot naturally creates a meditative state. There are a variety of walking meditations; but the following is very informal, simple, and will provide you with tremendous self-awareness.

When and Where

Meditation while walking of course is best practiced while outdoors. It is recommended that the setting for the walk be in natural surroundings, in order to make the most of the experience. Simply being in nature increases awareness and physiology. The feelings of the breeze, the singing of the birds, or seeing the wings of a butterfly in flight will wake something inside of you and energize you. Also, it is suggested that at least 20 minutes are set aside for just walking meditation, free of any distractions. The walk should be given your undivided attention, so that you can sink into the meditative experience fully.

Preparation

Before starting the walk, make sure you spend a little time to prepare while standing still. Use this opportunity to become aware of your body. Breathe deeply and inhale deep into your belly. Place your full attention focused on this sensation, while you allow your breathing to return to normal on its own. Take note of how your body is feeling while you are standing, and focus on all of the feelings going through your body too. This will help begin the meditative experience with increased awareness and concentration.

Walking Meditation

Begin by walking at a relaxed and moderately slow, but normal pace. There is no need to win a race while meditating. Focus on the sensations of your body while you are in motion. It is natural to find your attention drifting towards the beautiful sights around you; however, keep bringing the attention back to the internal of your body. Pay attention to the physical experience, and do not allow yourself to get caught up in thoughts or worries. Notice how your body feels in greater detail when you pay attention to the walking motions. Feel your entire body becoming involved in the action. Focus on the alternation of your left and right foot, along with the swinging of your arms and hips naturally.

Become aware of areas of your body that you typically are not aware of normally. Notice how your feet feel as they make contact with your socks and shoes. Feel the fabric's texture rubbing them, while feeling the weight of your body supported on them. Sense the entire foot, including the heel as it moves on the ground and how the movement rolls towards the ball of your foot and toes. Pay attention to the foot as it lifts and moves forward. Next, allow awareness to float into every other part of your body in the same way. Slowly, scan your ankles, calves, knees, thighs, hips, back, chest, shoulders, neck, arms, head, and even your skin. You can scan your body at random by moving your awareness from part to part, or you can systematically scan from your toes to your head.

Whenever you become conscious of any tension through your body, simply let it go. Let that part of your body become relaxed. Allow your hips and arms to swing loosely, while your body naturally takes over for walking. As you become more relaxed, the walking will become easier and more enjoyable. Remember, the most important thing is to focus your awareness consistently on your body. Whenever your mind starts to wander, reel it back in and regain your attention on the physicality your movements.

Also assuming you are walking in an area surrounded by nature take a look at your surroundings. Try to focus on which you find beauty in. Take some time to appreciate the beautiful plants and trees around you. Listen to the birds chirp away and notice if there are any other furry animals wondering about around you. I know for me there are usually a lot of ducks roaming around which I like to focus on and appreciate. Maybe it is close to fall and the leaves are starting to color really nicely. Whether it would be cute, fuzzy animals or plants and trees around you try and find something that you find beauty in and focus on that. When you focus on things that bring you pleasure you will find yourself to be more relaxed, making your meditative journey more profound and effective. This is why I recommend trying to find a nature like environment. I believe almost all of us can find some sort of beauty in something when surrounded by nature. Not to mention that the industrialized world can be very crazy and stressful at times, so being around nature is a great way to temporarily escape from that environment. This of course will then again help you relax and make your meditative experience more enjoyable and ultimately more effective as well.

Overall, walking meditation is an amazing way that you can transform something you do every day into a healing, nourishing, and enjoyable practice for awakening self-awareness. Do not worry if it feels a little awkward at first; keep going and stay focused. Little by little, it will begin to seem more natural and require less effort. With practice, walking meditation will lead to greater mindfulness and awareness. It will also help to relieve any symptoms of illness, lower high blood pressure, and relieve stress to improve your mood. Not to mention it is also good exercise as well.

Guide to Mindfulness Meditation

Mindfulness is a kind of meditation that involves focusing the mind on the present and developing a tranquil state of inner peace. Regular mindfulness meditation seeks to balance the stimuli coming from the surrounding environment with the stillness inside the soul. The resulting inner awareness helps people to navigate through hard times in their lives and brings clarity to everyday routines.

Mindfulness meditation is great for those of who live in a somewhat noisy or active environment and may find it difficult at times to find a place of complete solitude. The reason being is that mindfulness meditation is about using the environment around you to help you stay focused. While you don't want your environment to be too chaotic, as this may be too distracting, with mindfulness meditation it is okay to have a little bit of noise here and there.

So if you overhear your neighbors talking or you live near traffic and can hear a car drive by now and then it is fine. If all you can do is be alone in a single room or any place that is not overly distracting to the point that you can't get into the meditative mindset, then you should be good to go. The following is a guide into how you can practice mindfulness meditation and the benefits it will bring in your daily life.

Environment

The first step to effectively connect to your inner soul is through finding a sacred environment that will allow the clarity to take place. The ideal setting is a clean environment that is free from distractions and noises that will cause a loss of attention. Set aside a space that is devoted to your meditation. Make sure that only meaningful items that inspire you are in the space; clear away all unnecessary clutter. Your personal sacred environment can be in the corner of a room, or it can be outside under a tree in your backyard. Whatever space you choose, ensure that it is a place where you feel calm and comfortable.

Posture

Once you find a quiet and relaxing place for meditation, sit down in either a chair or directly on the floor. Your posture while you are sitting will dictate how the energy flows throughout your body; therefore, you need to assume a posture that will ensure clarity. Keep your head, neck, and back straight, but never stiff. Make sure your feet stay flat on the floor, your hips centered, and your spine straight up. It is helpful to envision that there is a string pulling your spine straight up like a puppet. Let your shoulders relax and relieve the tension. This posture will help develop a clear mind and create an optimal energy level for your meditative experience.

Focus

Of course, the central purpose of mindfulness meditation is to free your mind from all distractions and create a focused mind. In order to do this, it is suggested that you keep your attention on one object at a time. You could use a candle, a vase of fresh-cut roses, or another item that is sacred to you. Softly focus your gaze and undivided attention to one point on the object. This is going to be more difficult than you would think, but be patient with yourself and practice. Eventually, you will feel your energy shift as a state of calm washes over your body.

Breathing

Often times, we take our breathing for granted and do not pay much attention to it. However, mindfulness meditation strives for creating a focus on breathing because each breath is a connection with your spirit. Consciously focus on the sensation of the air as you inhale it in and exhale it out of your body. Feel the rise and fall of your chest, the air going through your nostrils, and it exiting through your mouth. Life is such a precious gift and breathing is what sustains us; so, focusing on the natural rhythm of your breathing will create a greater appreciation for every inhale and inner peace.

Thoughts

Pay attention to every thought that floats into your mind. Watch each thought come into your mind, then let it go. Whether it is a worry or a hope, do not suppress or ignore the thought. Instead, simply take note and label it as a thought. Stay calm and maintain the same slow breathing rate. If you ever feel yourself carried away with thoughts racing through your mind, examine what they are about. Remember to not be hard on yourself or make judgments if this should happen. It is normal and will actually help you become more aware of where your mind is at.

Mindfulness meditation can be ideal for many people who are looking for methods of personal and spiritual growth. It is perfect for individuals who live busy lives and have a difficult time focusing on the moment, without getting trapped in thoughts of the past or future. It can also be advantageous for chronic stress sufferers to reduce their anxiety and lower their blood pressure. Mindfulness can reap benefits for everyone though, such as greater emotional and physical well-being, improved immune functioning, and increased self-acceptance.

Taoist Meditation

Taoist meditation shares some commonalities with Hindu and Buddhist meditation systems; however, the Taoist method is a great deal less abstract and more down to Earth than the other highly contemplative traditions. After all, the meditative experience has no particular aim; it is an indirect meditation without established techniques or notions. Taoist meditation is solely focused upon the creation, transformation, and then transmission of an individual's inner energy. The following is an in-depth guide on the philosophy behind Taoist meditation and how it can be achieved.

Inner Peace Philosophy

Records indicate that breathing exercises associated with Taoist meditation have been practiced since 100 B.C., and they may go back even earlier than this.

Central to the Taoist meditation beliefs are the focus on correct breathing to allow the energy to flow throughout the body. The aim for its creation was to calm the mind and body from inconsequential thoughts, so that the individual can achieve their optimal strength.

Taoists emphasize two primary guidelines to their meditation, which referred to as jing and ding. Jing is the quiet and stillness, while ding is concentration and focus. They believe that combining these two together lets a person's attention turn inward and shut off all external senses that they call the "Five Thieves." Taoist meditation has the goal of developing awareness that is completely undistracted and an undifferentiated mind state. From there, individuals are able to experience perceptive insights naturally, feel enlightened by the flow of energy, and achieve inner peace.

How It Works

Although Taoist meditation is one of the simplest forms, it is often considered to be the most difficult. There are no required techniques or special postures that are necessary to achieve this pathless form of meditation. Instead, it is solely about experiencing the feelings and shifts in energy that arise. That being said, there are some steps that are useful to follow for Taoist meditation, but how you wish to conduct your own meditative experience is your choice.

One of the first steps is often to assume a comfortable sitting position, with a strong posture to support the body. It is often recommended to sit in the general direction of the sun. Rest your palms lightly on your thighs, above the knee. Straighten your spine and create an evenly balance of your weight. Begin by paying attention to the physical sensations of your body, such as the feel of the cold or warm breeze on your skin.

Once you have gained awareness at this level, shift your attention to your breathing and energy. Focus on the rate of your breathing, while treasuring the flow in and out of your lungs through the nostrils. Notice the flow of energy streaming in and out of vital points on your body, including between the eyebrows. Concentrate on the rising and falling of your chest, along with the expansion of your abdomen.

With your eyes half closed, envision a candle flame or a mandala before you. Focus on the center of the object, while taking in the edges with your peripheral eyesight. Concentrating in this fashion will help to dramatically erase all other distractions and thoughts entering your mind. In addition, some people find it helpful to recite mantras to harmonize the energy and gain awareness.

Taoists usually use three effective syllables, which are "Om," "Ah," and "Hum." Take notice of how the vibrations created with these mantras reach out to different energy points on your body. If your mind still keeps wandering, do not create judgment or negative energy by reprimanding yourself. Instead, visualize a sacred symbol or deity of personal significance to you to refocus your attention.

Overall, Taoist meditation requires daily practice in order to get the most from the meditative experiences. Taoist masters acknowledge that when you first begin, the mind is very uncooperative. It is believed that this is your emotional mind fighting against its extinction by the more powerful forces of spirituality. You must learn how to harness the senses and emotions of the mind, in order to release the inner spirit and energy to obtain deeper understanding.

Taoist meditation is renowned for its tremendous impact for stress relief and reducing the anxiety that lurks in every corner during our daily lives. Once you achieve energy, it can be supplied throughout your body to support improved health, longevity, and a transformation of the mind.

Zen Meditation

Zen meditation is associated with Buddhism, which places an emphasis on meditation as its core technique to unite the body with the mind. Its goal of the practice is to still the mind and focus, thus increasing the individual's self-awareness in the experience. Zen meditation achieves this goal by concentrating on erasing all thoughts from the mind, and focus on only the individual's posture and breathing. The following guide will offer a guide to Zen meditation, including the philosophy behind it, how to do it, and why you should give it a try.

Healing Philosophy

Zen meditation has its root within the Buddhist religion. According to the faith, all people possess a "Buddha Nature," which refers to an unlimited wisdom within. It is believed that this wisdom can only be accessed by experiencing the most natural state in the mind. Therefore, Zen meditation came about as the way to achieve this mental state, through tuning out the surrounding world and focusing on the inner nature of the soul. The religion believes wisdom should be acquired by building awareness, self observation, and practical experience, instead of through scriptures. Tapping into the "Buddha Nature" allows a deeper understanding of the world, others, and the self. Many people feel gifted with a completely new sense of knowledge and awareness. Buddhism teaches that Zen meditation enables individuals to find peace and harmony in the world. The form of meditation is believed to lead the person towards Satori, which is the first step towards reaching nirvana by awakening the true inner nature.

How It Works

Begin by finding a quiet, undisturbed location that would be ideal for meditation. It is usually the most beneficial to meditate in the early morning or late evening, depending on your personal preference. Whenever the time, ensure that you are not tired, since the last thing you want is to meditate to sleep. Also, dress comfortably in loose clothing that will not provide a distraction or restrict deep breathing. Gather a mat, small pillow, or cushion for comfort and support during the experience.

Now you are ready to begin Zen meditation. The first step to achieving a positive meditative experience is choosing the right position to sit in, and there are plenty to choose from. For example, there is the Full Lotus position, which is a stable position that involves you placing each of your feet up onto the opposite thigh. However, this position may be uncomfortable or downright painful for some people. There is a modification, the Half Lotus position, which includes putting the left foot onto the right thigh and placing the right leg under the left thigh. Make sure to do plenty of research to find the most beneficial position for your specific needs and optimize your experience. Once sitting, keep your back and spine erect in a strong posture.

Start clearing your mind of all errant thoughts and focus upon your natural breathing. You may keep your eyes open or shut them, depending on what works best for you. Focus on counting every inhale and exhale up to ten, and then start back at one. Your mind is likely to start wandering, so do not chastise yourself. Instead, acknowledge the thought and continue counting. Eventually, with practice you will not need to count and will just be able to concentrate naturally on the breaths. Do not be afraid to explore the stillness and uncover the hidden awareness within. Strive to meditate for fifteen minutes to begin with, and then increase the amount of time until you reach up to an hour.

Benefits

Even though the practice is highly linked with the Buddhist religious beliefs and traditions, you do not need to be a member of the religion to enjoy participating in Zen meditation and reap the wide variety of physical and mental benefits. It has been shown to reduce stress and anxiety significantly, while allowing the individual to cope with depression easier. It also improves posture, concentration, the immune system, and self-confidence. While it may be difficult to clear your mind to begin with, keep practicing and you will eventually experience a higher state of conscious that will greatly improve your overall health and well being.

Guided Meditation

Guided meditation allows the mind to be led on a particular journey, through focused contemplation and reflection. Individuals participating in this form of meditation often listen to a professional speak a guided meditation on a CD or record their own to play back. The key for having a successful experience is to let go of all thoughts clogging your mind, while letting the subconscious follow the spoken words. Your conscious mind falls asleep, so that the subconscious is pushed to the forefront and releases unconscious emotions.

Guided meditation involves an individual being guided verbally through the meditative experience to achieve relaxation and awareness. Since this form of meditation enables a meditator guided by either voice or a recording, it is one of the simplest methods to realize a deep state of inner stillness and peace.

Therefore, guided meditation is ideal for people who have difficulty staying focused and calm during meditative types. It also is perfect for those who need some assistance for direction on their inner journey or motivation to dig deeper past the surface.

How Guided Meditation Works

Guided meditation often takes place in a class with a meditation instructor, or at home by listening to a recording. In most cases, the guide asks the mediator to sit or lie down comfortably. The guide will then lead you through various visualizations and sensations that are meant for relaxation. While you relax with the guided meditation, your mind will become clearer and stress will fade away. In the deeply relaxed state, the subconscious of your mind will open up for an inner journey to improve any necessary aspects of your life.

Although some guided meditations are sometimes as

short as five minutes or as long as an hour, most will last for 15 minutes to a half hour. Some guides may incorporate tranquil classical music, but others may involve rock music. Guided meditations are often customized to meet individual goals, such as empowerment, positivity, or spiritual healing. At the conclusion, most guided meditators feel revitalized, relaxed, and emotionally refreshed with a whole new outlook. Below is a shortened example of a script that would resemble a guided meditation recording.

Guided Meditation Script Example:

Find a quiet place to sit down comfortably. Turn off the phone, dim the lights, and light some scented candles. Lay your hands loosely in your lap, let the tension leave your shoulders, and close your eyes. It is time to relax and be still without distractions. It is your time. Take a long breath, deep and slow. Hold it in for a moment, and then slowly let it go in an exhale.

Let yourself gradually sink into relaxation, like your toes are sinking in the sand on a beach. Allow the tension melt away as you breathe deeper with every breath. Take another slow, long breath in, hold it, and then breathe out. Empty all of the air out of your lungs on the exhale. Feel yourself start to drift into a deep stage of relaxation. Continue focusing on breathing slowly and soothingly. Let yourself relax and enjoy the sensations across your body.

Now, bring your focus to the crown of your head. Feel the relaxation begin to spread across your body, down from the top of your head. Allow the muscles in your temples, forehead, and face relax. Feel the relaxation spread down to your eyes, cheeks, and jaws. Let your facial muscles soften and let go of all the muscle pressure. Let the peaceful trance sensation flow down your neck, into your shoulders and releasing the tension for complete soothing. Breathe deeply.

While your body continues relaxing, let your mind clear and unwind. Feel the thoughts become weightless, floating through your mind like the leaves in the autumn breeze. Let the peace flow through your shoulders, chest, and abdomen. Feel your stomach slightly rise and fall with each breath, deeply and gently. Focus on the relaxation spreading along your back and down your spinal cord. Be aware of the peaceful sensations flowing all the way down to relax your buttocks.

Let the tension gradually flow out of the back and front of your thighs. Calm sensations then flow through your knees and into your calves. Relax your ankles and feet. Focus on releasing the tension from each of your ten toes. Your whole body is now the ultimate in relaxation and tranquility. Feel timeless, empty, and still. Enjoy the solitude and inner stillness. When thoughts enter your mind, simply set them free and return to your awareness. It will guide you home. Congratulate yourself for successfully taking the time to unwind.

Powerful Benefits of Guided Meditation

Guided meditations are unique because they will help you enter into a deep state of physical, emotional, mental, and even energetic balance. As a result, guided meditation will allow you to decrease anxiety, eliminate depression, reduce stress, improve your memory, and enhance your creativity.

In addition, physical benefits from guided meditation include reduced muscle tension, strengthened immune system functioning, lowered cholesterol levels, and decreased stress hormones. With this form of meditation, you can be guided towards increased feelings of vitality, positivity, and confidence to transform your life.

Therefore, guided meditation is ideal for individuals that are coping with depression, stress, anxiety, or low self-esteem. Through the deep contemplation, you will be able to replace the negative hard-wiring of the mind with increased positivity along the mental journey. Also through guided meditation, you will be capable of coping with stress easier and not spend so much time worrying. Instead, you can form a deep connection with your inner, spiritual self and release your subconscious mind.

Other Meditative Techniques

Although meditation is universal, there are a wide variety of meditation forms that vary from one another in different practices and goals as shown in the previous few chapters. Sometimes, it takes some tweaking in order to find the right technique that will suit an individual's personality and interests. The following are four more exceptional meditation practices that everyone should consider incorporating into their meditative experience for increased benefits.

Yoga Meditation

When yoga and meditation are combined together, they create a powerful tool that can significantly benefit the individual. The practice is ideal for those who are seeking new ways to improve their emotional, as well as their physical, well-being. It does so by bringing the body into a state of reflection and concentration. It promotes peace of thought, which is proven to reduce stress and the daily pressures of life. Through the body postures and mind cleansing exercises, yoga meditation provides relaxation, agility, and inner peace at the same time.

Individuals that practice yoga meditation on a regular basis experience tremendous benefits. Many people have found a decrease in high blood pressure, normalized pulse rates, and a boosted immune system. When you use it correctly, you will notice a decrease in illnesses and will easier fight off certain diseases. In addition, individuals that tend to fall into a negative mindset of hopelessness and uneasiness will realize increased levels of happiness, and self-awareness.

Tai Chi

Although it was originally designed for self-defense, tai chi is evolving into a form of meditative exercise that is useful for reducing stress and anxiety levels greatly. Affectionately referred to as meditation in motion, tai chi entails the series of movements that are performed in a slow, attentive manner. Combined with deep breathing exercises, it is a gentle form of exercise and stretching that maintain constant motion of the body. Since it is low impact, tai chi is ideal for individuals that are suffering from certain physical ailments, such as arthritis or chronic pain.

Including tai chi in your exercise regimen and meditative experience will result in many positive benefits to improve overall health. You will notice an increased amount of energy, stamina, flexibility, balance, agility, aerobic capacity, and muscle strength. In addition, tai chi will help enhance your quality of sleep, boost the immune system, decrease stress levels, and improve joint pain. There are many tai chi classes available in communities today, so it is recommended that you look into signing up to learn more from an instructor and be welcomed into a class setting for added socialization.

Transcendental Meditation

Also called TM, this form of meditation is geared towards individuals that are seeking a way to improve their self-awareness and unclog their minds from distracting thoughts. While meditating, individuals sit in a comfortable position with their eyes closed and repeat mantras. Through the experience, the ordinary mental processes become transcended to a state of pure consciousness.

You will be able to achieve perfect stability, order, calmness, and freedom from mental boundaries restricting your thoughts. Benefits associated with TM include clearer thinking patterns, increased overall health and longevity, reduced chronic pain, lower anxiety levels, and reduced risk for cardiovascular diseases.

As you can see, there are a variety of options available to choose from. It is recommended that you conduct further research on these alternatives, plus any others, in order to find the appropriate fit for your lifestyle. When you stumble upon the right one, it will be like the last piece of the puzzle clicking in and your health will soar.

How to Meditate to Help You Fall Asleep

If you are someone who has trouble sleeping there is no doubt that meditation can help with that. But there are actually meditating techniques that you can use that are strictly for helping you to fall asleep. The following section is going to show you how you can use meditation to help you fall asleep. I broke it down in 4 easy steps.

Step 1:

First it is very important to sit comfortably. Your bed would actually be a good choice. It is not normally recommended to sit in your bed when you meditate as one can fall asleep from being too relaxed, but since falling asleep is the end goal here, you're bed seems to be the ideal place to sit for this technique.

Step 2:

Now you want to focus on something. A lit candle would be great, but any spot along the wall would be fine as well. Make sure it is around eye level or even slightly above is fine too. Now slowly breathe in and out with your belly expanding as you breathe in and contracting as you breathe out. Pretty much like when you would normally breathe when meditating.

Start to notice how your muscles are becoming relaxed. Also notice your eyelids starting to get heavy. You may even want to start to scan your body from your toes to your head. As you scan through your body, notice how each particular muscle starting to relax. Feel the tension releasing out of them as you exhale from each breath. Once you are done notice how your eye lids are starting to get heavy. Now start counting down the breaths you take from 10. Once

you are finished counting, close your eyes and notice
how calm and peaceful you feel.

Step 3:

Now close your eyes and imagine yourself going
down an escalator or walking down a flight of stairs.
As you are descending, count down from 20. I like to
imagine myself going down in darkness. Once you
finish counting down and fully descended from the
stairs or elevator start walking forward.

Step 4:

Now as you are walking forward, imagine yourself
walking through a forest at night. Notice how peaceful
it is all around you. Hear the crickets chirping and the
noise from the other night critters such as the owl.
Feel the nice cool breeze gently blowing up against
you. Slowly keep on walking forward down a nature
trail.

Eventually as you walk down imagine the nature trail lead off to a nice beach. In the middle of the sand you find a nice cozy sleeping bag right next to a camp fire. As you lay down listen to the waves gently swaying along the ocean. At this point count down slowly from 10. Once you finish snap back to realty; turn off the lights and go to bed. You should be very relaxed and have not trouble falling asleep at this point.

One last thing for me to point out is that you can switch sceneries if you like with something else. Perhaps you like the beach but do not feel at peace in a forest. The point of this is that you want to imagine yourself in a scene that brings calmness and peacefulness to you. So whatever that is go ahead and substitute that in.

Final Thoughts

This book has shown various meditation techniques that you can start using today. I wanted to come up with as many as possible to make sure I appeal to everyone. There is most certainly some technique here for everyone. You may want to try them all to see which one you like best. This is fine, however I imagine you focus on learning and mastering one technique at a time. You don't want to overwhelm yourself.

You may also only end up trying one or two techniques in this book as well too. This is also okay. The key is to find what works best for you and do it. I mentioned this before but it is really worth repeating. The only way you can fail to meditate is simply fail to try. There is no one absolute way. You may even take one of the techniques and make slight modifications to it because you find it works best for you.

Whatever you have to do go, ahead and do it. As long as you start and dedicate yourself to doing it on a regular basis, you are already on your way to mastering the art of meditation. Now with that get started and start living a more calm, peaceful, and fulfilling life now!

Other Books by Max Fischwell:

Free Yourself from the Shackles of Clutter:

Simple + Easy Ways to Declutter Your Home + Other Vital Aspects of Your Life

Free Yourself from the Shackles of Negative Thinking:

Eliminate the 7 Positive Killers and Start Living a Fulfilled Life Now

Yoga 101:

Simple Yoga Poses to Calm Your Mind & Energize Your Body

Other Recommended Reading:

Meditation for Dummies by Stephan Bodan:

8 Minute Meditation by Victor Davich:

How to Quiet Your Mind by Marc Allen:

How to Meditate in Just 2 Minutes

by Phil Pierce:

Made in the USA
Lexington, KY
01 April 2014